Unlimited Willpower

UNLIMITED WILLPOWER

HOW TO MAKE 2021 THE BEST YEAR OF YOUR LIFE

Joseph Abell

ISBN: 9798596913637

First edition, 2020.
www.joseph.coach

Dedication

This book is dedicated to Alfred, the man who taught me to create my own fire.

Table of Contents

Acknowledgements

Over the last few years, I have been gifted with friendships that inspired me to become a better person. Thank you Jonathan, Christian, Alex, and Destiny Rose. Because of you, my life is in full bloom.

Chapter 1
Your Ascended Self

You Already Know your Path

You know, better than anyone, who you could be. You've seen yourself at your absolute best. You know all your talents and interests and experiences.

In your head, there is a fuzzy image of your Ascended Self, the version of you that makes all the right choices. Your Ascended Self:

- Acts with certainty and confidence.
- Is proud of every aspect of their life.
- Doesn't turn back when things get hard.

Take a moment to think of something that your Ascended Self does that you don't currently do. Examples: working out regularly, giving 100% at work, getting straight As.

Seriously, think of one. It just takes a moment.

Now think of something that you currently do that your Ascended Self *doesn't* do. Examples: abusing alcohol or drugs, staring at a screen all day, hanging out with toxic people.

For real, though. Think of one.

I'm guessing you had no trouble thinking of how your Ascended Self is different from the person you are now. Yes, your Ascended Self is wiser. But that's not what really sets them apart. You already have a good picture of who you should be – but for some reason, you're not that person. That means you're making choices that you *know* aren't good for you. You're consciously giving up on your Ascended Self and allowing yourself to be something less than excellent.

You're not doing what you know you should be doing.

How can that be? How could you know what do and then just not do it? Is something horribly wrong with you?

It's completely normal to fall short of your Ascended Self. But you don't have to tolerate it for another day. This book is not about how to live your best life. It's about why *you're not already living it.*

The Trauma of Wasted Potential

You have a drive to be excellent that is intrinsic to who you are. Every sapient being carries it. Like a conscience, it can be suppressed – but it makes itself known in other ways.

You can tell yourself that you're fine with the life you have, or that you're tired of trying and failing. But every day that you tolerate the non-excellent version of yourself, you get a glimpse of your Ascended Self in the corner of your eye. It taunts you. It calls to you. And when you deny it, you feel something deep inside you rip just a little bit – like a few threads tearing at the edge of a blanket. Over time, those tiny rips shred you to tatters. You're exhausted and ashamed. The only thing you know to do about it is to distract yourself. But you can never distract yourself so much that the pain goes away. Your Ascended Self never stops calling to you, because you know that it's never too late to become that person.

Collapsing in front of the TV with your favorite junk food is supposed to feel relaxing. But it's not - not *really* – because you can still hear your Ascended Self calling to you from the other room. The more you try to shut it out, the more exhausted you become. There is nowhere to hide from the shame of letting yourself down.

Turning your back on your own greatness cuts you off from one of the most valuable and rewarding things you can experience in this life: self-respect.

That's why you must try again. Even though you doubt, even though you failed, even though you're tired. The only alternative is a lifetime of shame and unhappiness. You're never truly going to be able to live with yourself unless you return to the base of the mountain, look up, and start climbing.

But this time, things are going to be different. This time, every step will build learned confidence instead of self-doubt, because you'll have the secret of unlimited willpower.

Chapter 2
The Vicious Cycle

High Ambitions

You're ready to make some personal changes. Motivation is high. You're kicking things up a notch at work; you're committing to a workout plan; you're changing your diet; you're cutting certain foods or drinks from your diet; you're getting into a daily meditation practice.

You're proud of the person you have chosen to become. You tell your friends and family about it. You announce it on social media. There's no going back now, you think. This is the new you. You're going to be fully ascended from now on!

- The alarm clock goes off on day one.

You hop out of bed for a healthy breakfast and meditation. You crush it at work. You stave off cravings for unhealthy food. You get a good workout in and go to bed on time, tired but happy.

- The alarm clock goes off on day two.

You climb out of bed and stare at the wall for a minute, reminding yourself of the person you have chosen to be. You eat a healthy breakfast and meditate. You crush it at work. At lunch, the cravings are overwhelming. You sneak a little of the food that you said you wouldn't eat. You get a decent workout in and go to bed tired. The excitement is already fading fast. You wonder: Why was today so much harder than yesterday? Is your motivation really that fickle? You beat yourself up until you fall asleep.

- The alarm clock goes off on day ten.

You drag yourself out of bed and eat a healthy breakfast while staring at your phone. You skip the meditation. You go to work and do the sort of adequate job the "old you" used to do. But somehow, even though you're not working as hard, you're more exhausted than ever. On the way home, you pull over and pick up a bunch of the food you said you wouldn't eat. You find a way to justify it to yourself. "I deserve it," you think.

You plop down in front of Netflix and graze on junk food, scrolling social media, feeling less and less rested by the moment.

- The alarm clock goes off on day twenty.

You disable it and go back to sleep.

Teaching Yourself to Fail

Think about something that you're good at. It can be anything that you're confident you can do well, even something seemingly trivial like whistling, building Minecraft castles or riding a bike. If I asked you to do that thing for me right now, you'd confidently say that you could. If you made a New Year's resolution to do it every day, you'd probably have no problem following through on it. You know that because you've already done it successfully many times. That doesn't just build confidence, that *is* confidence.

Confidence is memory of past success.

I'm not talking about the naïve enthusiasm of a child who hasn't experienced much success or failure. They charge into a new activity without thinking about whether they'll succeed. They're just doing.

But once you've had enough life experience, that innocence fades away. Whenever you think about yourself doing something new, you compare it to what you've done in the past. You ask yourself: "Have I done anything similar? How did that go?"

Suppose I ask you to join me on a two-day cross-country hike. This will be a difficult trek across steep terrain. You think back to past hikes you've been on. In one, you got lost and had to be rescued by a search party. In another, you were mauled by a mountain lion. In another, you fell and sprained your ankle when you were still in sight of the trailhead. So now, the prospect of another hike fills you with consternation. You feel certain that you will fail. You're experiencing self-doubt, the opposite of confidence.

Self-doubt is memory of past failure.

Failure is part of life. So is sticking with something until you get good at it. But when you set out to do something and fail – not an expected failure, like falling while learning to ride a bike, but a genuine failure, like bombing a job interview – it changes how you see yourself. You're teaching yourself that you are bad at doing that thing, and that the next time you try it, you'll fail again.

This is particularly dangerous when it comes to self-improvement. When you make big personal changes and then fail at them, you're teaching yourself a terrible lesson. You're not just saying: "I'm bad at working out consistently." You're saying: "I'm bad at making positive changes in my life."

Failing repeatedly at personal growth becomes a poison in your heart. Your enthusiasm wanes. Then comes that terrible, soul-tearing desync: you start seeing ways you can improve your life *and then not doing them.* You're not holding back because you're unmotivated, but because you don't believe that you can successfully make that change in the long term. Your self-doubt is so crippling that it's keeping you from even starting.

This isn't a generic hesitance that can be fixed with a motivational speech. It's an informed doubt built on direct life experience. You know you can't change your life because you already tried and failed.

Still, you want to be a better person. Sometimes the motivation comes back, or you find something excitingly positive and productive.

You choose to believe again. You fail again. And you fall even lower than before.

The self-doubt piles on top of you, layer after layer, until the weight of it crushes you. There's an impenetrable barrier separating you from your Ascended Self. You don't know how to do anything but give up.

This is the Vicious Cycle:

1. Live in a way that you're ashamed of
2. Genuinely try to change
3. Fail and slip back into your old pattern
4. Teach yourself that you can't change
5. Live in a way that you're ashamed of again – but now you're even more ashamed, and you stay there for even longer

Good intentions and knowledge can't break this cycle. To make this the best year of your life, we'll need to identify the real reason you keep failing. We need to talk about your willpower.

Chapter 3
How Willpower Really Works

The Lucky Elite

The mainstream understanding of willpower views it as a fundamental trait, like being extroverted or sensitive. We're told that some people just *have* high willpower. The stars aligned; they got the right genes or the right soul or listened to Mozart when they were kids, and now they have that "something-

something." They're crushing life thanks to their awesome willpower.

Since you're not achieving as much as them, it follows that you're not one of those lucky few. Perhaps that's why you keep failing at personal growth. You try to act like a high-willpower person, but you can't keep up the charade forever.

Here's the first powerful secret I want to give you. It's one that changed my life and helped me tap into my infinite potential. The secret is this:

Willpower is not a character trait.

Everyone's capacity for willpower is basically the same. It's not how much we start with, but how we spend and recover it that makes all the difference.

Willpower Knows Nothing

Willpower can't tell the difference between a donut and a carrot. It doesn't know sleeping in or waking up early; it doesn't know where or who you are. It doesn't know what's good for you. Growing as a person and making good choices doesn't intrinsically cost willpower.

In fact, acting destructively can cost willpower. If you're a driver, it has probably occurred to you at some point that you could total your vehicle and badly hurt yourself with a simple flick of the wrist at the wrong moment. It would be physically easy to do. But it would also require tremendous willpower because you would have to override your innate survival instinct.

That's because willpower isn't governed by what's good or bad for you, it's governed by *what you change.*

Willpower is the ability to consciously change your default behavior.

Maybe you've decided to stop using social media after dark. This is a change because social media has been a big part of your evenings for the last few years. Today, you come home late and automatically pull out your phone. Then you remember: *I don't use social media after dark.* You're going to have to resist your default behavior. You spend some willpower to put your phone away.

That's all willpower is: the ability to resist your default behavior. Knowing that has huge implications for your ability to make 2021 unlike any year you've experienced.

Real Life Mana Bar

There's a common mechanic in gaming called the mana bar. It's a supply of mental or magical energy that you can spend to use your character's abilities. Perhaps you cast a big spell that depletes most of your mana. You'll now have to wait as it slowly regenerates before you can cast it again.

This is a perfect representation of how willpower works.

- Your alarm goes off. **Your default behavior is to keep sleeping.** You spend some willpower to get out of bed.
- You go to the kitchen. **Your default behavior is to eat junk food.** You spend some willpower to eat healthy instead.
- You finish breakfast. **Your default behavior is to scroll social media.** You spend some willpower to meditate instead.

Every time you resist your default, you expend some willpower. By the end of a typical day in January full of New Year's resolutions, you've badly depleted your willpower. Your mana bar is empty. You collapse in bed, and as you sleep, it regenerates. You wake up with your bar back up to 60%.

You spend your reduced reserve of willpower until it runs out. By now, you're spiritually and emotionally exhausted. You're struggling to make any decisions at all. You're moving in a haze. All you can muster now is your default behavior.

Have you struggled with motivation throughout your life? Maybe. But I'm willing to bet without even meeting you that most of the problems you blamed on motivation can actually be traced to poor willpower management. You are a finite person trying to act infinite – like a video game character using cheat codes.

That's great news for you because it means you can do something about it. If willpower were a character trait, you'd simply have to accept a deficit as your lot in life. But since it's a resource, changing how you manage it can change everything. It can allow you to break the Vicious Cycle and succeed where you repeatedly failed.

The Currency of Ascension

When you're aware of willpower as a resource that you spend to change your behavior, you see the world in an entirely new way. You can think of every action that breaks from your default as having a specific willpower cost.

Sometime soon – probably today – you're going to desync from your Ascended Self. You'll do something that makes you feel a little sheepish. Here's what I want you to do when that happens.

Don't be hard on yourself. There's no need for that. Just mentally note it to yourself. Like this: "I should go to bed, but I'm not going to bed. That means going to bed costs more willpower than I currently have. Going to bed is pretty easy, so my willpower bar must be depleted."

The more you observe your behavior in terms of willpower costs, the easier it becomes. You'll notice a point in each day when your bar empties and you start coasting. You'll notice what depletes you and what recharges you. You'll be able to directly observe yourself making decisions, which unlocks the ability to change them for good.

Chapter 4
Make Good Behavior Easy

Discounts over Time

You can't intrinsically change how much willpower you can access, but you can change how much you have to spend to be the person you want to be.

Remember: making good choices doesn't cost willpower; *change* costs willpower. That means every day that you make the same choice, it becomes more normal and the cost of making that choice again goes down.

If you can string together many days in a row of the same behavior, it will become the default.

The first day that you don't open social media after dark, you spend 15% of your willpower reserve. A week later, it only costs 10%. Six months later, it costs 1%. Six years later, it's free. That's right: the thing that once required conscious willpower to do is now *automatic*.

Making the same choice over and over eventually reduces its willpower cost to zero.

We all have that one friend or family member who works way too hard. Maybe you are that person. This overachiever feels a responsibility to everyone else. There's a fire under them that pushes them out of bed and keeps them going until they collapse. As they fall asleep, they mentally review all the things they failed to do that day and vow to push themselves even harder the next day.

Suppose that person is given an all-expenses-paid tropical vacation. Seven days without a care in the world, just relaxing on the beach. That should be easy! All they have to do is show up and relax. But for this person, the prospect of seven unproductive days fills them with anxiety. All they can do is think about everything that must be going wrong in their absence, and how they're letting everybody down. They'll have to strongly resist their default to get through this vacation.

If your default behavior is work, resting requires willpower.

This is the first big key to unlocking your best year ever. Whatever behavior you want to implement will cost a lot at first, but if you stick with it, it will eventually feel so natural that you will actually have to expend willpower to stop.

- Imagine being someone who has to *try* not to work out.
- Imagine being someone who has to *try* to sleep in.
- Imagine being someone who has to *try* to tolerate toxic behavior.

Aligning with your Ascended Self will take a long time and a lot of hard work. But it won't always be difficult. Your Ascended Self isn't someone who is so motivated that they exert massive amounts of willpower every day. They're someone who has to expend little-to-no willpower to make the right choices.

Unlimited willpower is unlocked when being your Ascended Self costs less willpower than you're recharging.

What could the version of you who automatically makes good choices accomplish? Who could you become if you lived excellently all day and felt rested and refreshed at the end?

Discounts from Environment

Decisions are complicated. Your default behavior isn't a simple yes/no decision; it's a product of a variety of factors including your past experiences, personality, and environment.

For example, your default behavior might be to eat junk food as soon as you get home. But you *also* have a default behavior to eat and drink things that are already in your kitchen. So, if you open the fridge and there's no junk food in there, you'll actually have to spend some willpower to go out and buy more. If the cost of putting your shoes back on is high enough, you'll skip the junk food even if you have no willpower left to eat healthier.

You'll still have to resist buying more tomorrow. But the simple act of emptying your fridge significantly reduced the willpower cost of the behavior you wanted.

Your surroundings drastically change willpower cost.

This is why stores are arranged to make you walk past a bunch of impulse buys like magazines and breath mints. Maybe you wouldn't actively seek them out, but now they're in arm's reach. All you have to do is toss it onto the conveyor! The willpower cost of buying it is now incredibly low.

If you start impulse buying, that will eventually become your default behavior. You'll have to exert willpower every time you check out if you want to stop.

The Arrival Hack

If you put yourself in places where you do what you're trying to quit (like on the couch when you're cutting down on TV), the willpower cost to resist will be high. If you put yourself in places where you do what you're trying to do (like sit down at the desk where you study), the willpower cost to act will be low. You can harness this to "hack" your behavior, even if your willpower reserve is low. The hack is elegant in its simplicity.

Instead of committing to a behavior, commit to showing up.

For example, you may be struggling with establishing good sleep habits. Your mind fights you when you think about looking away from a screen. You committed to 8 hours of sleep, but now you're overwhelmed. The willpower cost is too high!

So instead, you commit to switching to your pajamas and getting into bed. You remind yourself that you can still stare at your phone when you're there, so the willpower cost is greatly reduced. Of course, once you're in bed with the lights off, you're likely to fall asleep much faster than you otherwise would have.

Instead of committing to a workout regimen, you might commit simply to going to the gym and putting on your workout clothes.

That's it! If you immediately change out of them again and leave, you've still upheld your commitment to yourself. Of course, once you're at the gym and ready to go, the willpower cost will have dropped way down. You'll find it quite easy to start working out.

- Instead of a word count, commit to opening your book file every day.
- Instead of changing your diet, commit to tracking what you eat – whatever it winds up being.
- Instead of restricting your screen time, commit to looking away from your phone and taking one deep breath before you check a social media app.

If you keep showing up day after day, putting yourself in the environment where making the right choice is easy, taking the next step will become more and more affordable in terms of willpower.

To make this work, you need to truly count arrival as upholding your commitment.

Don't allow yourself to feel ashamed if you walk out of the gym immediately. You committed to showing up, and you did. That's success.

Don't make the arrival hack your first plan whenever you make a change. But if you're struggling to implement a change and you're looking for an easier first step, or you're feeling overwhelmed and you're struggling to stay on course, this can really help.

Chapter 5
You are an Animal

There's a can of worms waiting to be opened here: we want to figure out what's instinct, what's part of your essential self, what's part of your upbringing and social programming, and so on. That's a fascinating topic, but we don't need to wade into it for you to unlock unlimited willpower this year.

So, let's simplify and just say this:

Some behaviors will always cost at least some willpower.

In other words: no matter how faithfully you repeat certain behaviors, you'll never be able to get the willpower cost all the way down to zero.

Avoiding junk food is a good example. If you avoid processed, greasy, sugary meals for long enough, your preferences will change. Carrots will start to taste sweet. You'll enjoy the nutty flavor of oatmeal. If you're really faithful, you'll get to a point where a bag of chips or a tray of cookies are unappetizing to you. They'll barely register as food. But even if you stay the course for twenty years, the cost of avoiding it will still be a little higher than zero.

Here's why.

The human body is not designed for a life of electric lights. It doesn't know that grocery stores exist. It is designed for a much simpler lifestyle – hunting and gathering, travelling from place to place, using simple tools. Your body thinks that you may have to go for long periods of time without eating. It also assumes that you are constantly in a caloric deficit.

If your ancient ancestor found a berry patch and tasted the sugar in the fruit, their response would be to immediately eat as much of it as they could, pick the rest, and bring it back to the tribe to share. They passed that instinct down to you. So, when you bite into a brownie, your brain lights up with excitement. You feel like you've found something rare that will help you delay starvation. Your impulse is to eat as much of it as possible, as quickly as possible.

For all your good discipline and good intentions, you can't rewire that instinct. All you can do is manage it.

Your instincts have a lot of wisdom and can save you in dangerous situations. But they're also poorly equipped for modern society. You have to navigate a world full of products and experiences that are specifically designed to take advantage of your instincts – to raise the willpower cost of good behavior so high that you are powerless to resist.

Here are 5 ways to fight back.

1. Avoid Triggers

If you're avoiding sugar, don't go into Starbucks. If you're getting over your ex, block them and delete your pictures of them and take a break from playlists full of love songs. Don't make your willpower costs higher than they have to be.

2. Don't Brag in Advance

Telling people about what you're going to achieve feels good – *too* good. That's because your mammal brain can't tell the difference between the dopamine rush of genuine achievement, and the rush of congratulations in advance. The more praise you get now, the less is waiting for you at the finish line and the less you drive you have to get there.

That doesn't mean you can't talk about the positive changes you're making. It just means you need to change how you talk about them. Limit yourself to only talking about what you have already done. For example, instead of saying: "I'm never vaping again," say: "I haven't vaped in 3 days." That's real. You already did it and you deserve to feel good about it.

The struggle will continue tomorrow. When you get to the end of tomorrow without vaping, you can be proud about that, too.

3. Stay Vigilant

Some behaviors will eventually become automatic. Once they do, you can relax and make exceptions without worrying that you're derailing your progress. But with instinct-controlled behaviors, a moment of indulgence can significantly increase the willpower cost of good behavior. It'll get easier and easier, but you'll still have to be at least somewhat disciplined for the rest of your life.

4. Fight Instinct with Instinct

If you're compulsively using your phone past your bedtime because of your instinctive drive to win social approval, consciously tap into your competing instinctive drive to sleep. Focus your awareness on that feeling. Tell yourself that you're powerless to resist the urge to go to bed.

5. Indulge When You're Strong

If you're feeling good and your willpower bar is full, indulging may not be that dangerous. You'll be able to handle the temptation that follows. But if you're exhausted, the upcoming willpower battle will be too much to handle. You'll slide into a binge and give up on yourself.

This isn't the same as: "I've been good, so I deserve this cookie." If your goodness has depleted your willpower, that cookie is going to set you back. Instead, make sure you're able to say: "I am strong, so I can handle this cookie."

That means you're going to need to create big reserves of willpower that you can spend to change your behavior and maintain a surplus at all times so you can navigate day-to-day temptations. That brings us to the next chapter.

Chapter 6
Recharge your Willpower

At the heart of the Vicious Cycle is a simple equation: you're spending more willpower than you're recovering. That means you're constantly running on empty, which means you don't have the energy to consistently resist yourself when you want to.

Building a Virtuous Cycle will require that you recharge your willpower every single day. Sadly, you can't drink a potion to instantly refill your willpower bar. The process is a bit more complicated.

Passive Regeneration

At any given moment, you're either spending willpower or gaining it. When you're scrolling Instagram in bed at midnight or doing a mindless part of your job, your willpower is slowly regenerating because you're not resisting your default behavior.

Passive regeneration is a slow process. It doesn't recharge you fast enough to sustain meaningful life changes like starting a workout routine or improving your grades. It helps, but you're going to need a lot more to make 2021 the best year of your life.

Active Regeneration

You can rapidly restore your willpower with rest — but not just any rest. In 2021, the forms of rest that you're likely to default to don't actively regenerate you.

These include:

- Binging TV
- Playing video games
- Scrolling social media
- Reading/watching most news

All of these activities engage the consuming part of your brain. Sure, you're inactive. Sure, you're defaulting to behavior you didn't feel like you had to choose. But your mind isn't truly *resting*.

Just because you're inactive doesn't mean you're resting.

Contrast with restorative rest such as:

- Walking in nature

- Playing with animals
- Meditation
- Yoga

These allow you to get into the sort of quiet, present headspace that rapidly recharges your willpower.

Interestingly, *how* you experience something can be just as important as *what* you experience. For example, playing music in the background while you do something else probably won't recharge you. Putting on a good set of headphones, closing your eyes, and focusing on it can.

Changing How You Rest

That doesn't mean you should cut all of these non-restorative behaviors out; many of them have other value. Maybe you watch TV with your family. You stay connected to a distant friend with video games. You use social media to build your platform. Playing music in the background helps you focus. You read the news because you care.

None of these behaviors are fundamentally bad, but you need to be aware that they aren't recharging you. Use them intentionally for play or productivity – don't use them to rest.

If your willpower isn't recharging fast enough, you'll get big gains from switching from a non-restorative inactive behavior to genuine rest.

The annoying catch: changing how you rest will *require* willpower at first, which means you'll actually feel more depleted in the short term. Give yourself time to adjust before you start using your new willpower reserves on other things.

Now here's where things get tough.

Distraction Dependence

Many people – especially younger generations – live every waking day without a single second of genuine rest. They are either working, distracted, or both from the moment they wake until the moment they fall asleep. If you are one of those people, creating even two minutes of actual rest in your day will require enormous willpower. Here's why:

Restorative rest doesn't distract you from your own thoughts.

Why is it so difficult to put down the phone for a few minutes and watch clouds? It's not because clouds are boring, it's because they can't distract you.

When you're desynced from your Ascended Self, a cloud of unpleasant thoughts forms around you: feelings of inadequacy, worrying about the future, playing an imaginary conversation over and over. This dark cloud swirls around you constantly, searching for a way inside.

Thanks to the smartphone, you can keep your mind slightly engaged at all times so your mind never has a moment to itself. The moment you step into an elevator or pull up to a stop light, you can reach for your phone and immediately pull up something that blocks out the dark cloud. You can live your entire life like this — desperately consuming, running away from your Ascended Self, not allowing your shame or regret to whisper to you for even a second.

But if you do that, your willpower won't recharge properly. You won't have enough to become the person you want to do be. The trauma of wasted potential will hurt more every day. You'll become even more dependent on your distractions — because now they're keeping you from thinking about how much of your life you've lost to your distractions. Every day, the willpower cost of putting your phone down will build higher.

If you distract yourself long enough, the emotional toll of 5 seconds of silence will terrify you.

The harder but far more productive path is to stop running. Turn off the distractions with the specific intention of allowing yourself to feel bored or disappointed. Let your Ascended Self speak. Open the door to the bad feelings. Deal with your trauma. Let go of the past. Make peace with your fears.

Don't get me wrong: that's a long and complex journey. Taking it goes way beyond the scope of this book. For now, just know this: it's okay to feel bad.

If you've become highly dependent on distractions, a 2-minute meditation will take all the willpower you can muster. You won't feel peace from it, you'll feel anxious and stressed. But you'll stick with it, and the next day will take a little less of a toll. You'll keep meditating, conserving willpower in other areas of your life so you don't slip up.

You'll confront the darkness and survive. You'll stop being afraid of it. This will break your dependence on distractions, allowing you to use social media or binge TV when you choose to, rather than because you're afraid not to.

It will allow you to build a schedule full of genuine rest, filling you with unprecedented levels of willpower.

And it will give you the chance to work through the things in your heart that are blocking your happiness.

You already know that you shouldn't be a slave to the screen. You don't have to go cold turkey! Movies, TV, the internet, social media, games – they're all incredible innovations that can add a lot to your life when used correctly. Just please understand: taking control of your relationship with your distractions is a critical first step in breaking the Vicious Cycle and having your best year ever. If you skip it, nothing else will produce the results that you want.

Chapter 7
Go to Sleep

Sleep Matters

Your body repairs itself and builds muscle while you sleep. Your mind processes what you experienced that day and stores it in long-term memory.

Sleep is essential to your survival. Get enough of it, and you'll be fully functional. Get a lot of it, and you'll be unstoppable.

"Roger Federer and LeBron James have said they sleep an average of **12 hours per**

day," ESPN reported in 2012 (emphasis added). "Usain Bolt, Venus Williams, Maria Sharapova and Steve Nash sleep up to 10 hours per day. Most NBA players take naps every game day, sometimes for as long as 3 hours."[1]

Modern professional athletes consider sleep to be just as critical as what they're doing in the gym or on the court to prepare. It is almost impossible to overstate its importance.

Sleep is the single most efficient way to restore your willpower.

If you're not sleeping well, this is your starting point on the journey to unlimited willpower.

"But Joseph," you object, "I'm special. I can actually get by on just a few hours and feel fine."

Maybe.

Maybe that's true.

Or maybe you're not special. Maybe you've gone without good sleep for so long that you can't remember what it feels like to wake up rested. Maybe you're limping along, using high doses of stimulants, zoning out throughout the day, overwhelmed by even the most pedestrian of tasks. Maybe you're lying to yourself so you can stay up all night doing nothing.

You're the only one who truly knows your situation. If you're one of the exceptional humans who can function at 100% on less sleep, more power to you. But you're probably not – and the only person you're fooling is yourself.

I'm sure you have good excuses. Your job, school, family, neighborhood, medication, condition, whatever. You may not be able to change those things. But you do need to acknowledge that your lack of sleep is holding you back — because if you don't, you'll keep failing and you won't understand why.

The Rise of Insomnia

In prehistoric times, the sun went down below the horizon for about half the day. Dangerous predators came out and the air cooled. If you were awake, you had to feed a fire that produced a pleasing crackle and a flickering yellow light. Prehistoric people probably had no trouble sleeping.

Today, you're surrounded by steady white/blue light and screens and loud noises. If you choose, you don't ever have to experience darkness again. Addictive activities are constantly competing for your attention, and you can indulge them for free until you physically pass out.

1 in 3 Americans don't get enough sleep.[2] If you're one of them, you're in good company.

Yes, it will require willpower at first to create good sleep habits. But you'll start seeing massive returns almost immediately. Prioritize your sleep.

Create Sleep Opportunity

Going to sleep is more involved than just making the decision and closing your eyes. It's a process with many steps. If you don't plan for it, those steps usually begin at the time that you should actually be in bed. Along the way, you might get distracted or return to a screen – and suddenly, you're an hour past your bedtime and still wide awake.

Create a part of your day that is dedicated to getting into sleep mode.

That means brushing your teeth, flossing, changing into pajamas, removing your makeup. If you shower before bed, that's part of the process, too.

Tonight, time your routine from the moment you start "winding down" to the time that you're in bed with the lights off and your eyes closed. This is time you need to protect if you want to recharge enough willpower to transform your life.

We'll go into more detail on morning and evening routines in the next chapter. First, let's talk about a few ways to upgrade your habit so good sleep becomes automatic. Remember that all these changes require willpower to implement. Pace yourself. Don't do it all at once!

Have a Bedtime

This is simple math.

T = *Hours it takes to create sleep opportunity*

8 = *Hours you want to be asleep*

A = *Time you want to wake up*

$$A - (T + 8) = \text{Bedtime}$$

Suppose you want to wake up at 6 AM and your evening ritual takes one hour.

$$6\ \text{AM} - (1 + 8) = 9\ \text{PM}$$

If you have unhealthy sleep habits right now, carving out 9-10 hours to give to sleep will be difficult. You'll feel like you're losing a chunk of your life. In fact, the opposite will be true: you'll reclaim a big chunk of the day that you were previously on autopilot.

Make the commitment to yourself. I promise you that the rewards will be worth it.

Sleep in the Dark

Your body is designed to respond to light. Prepare your room for sleep by closing the windows and turning off all the lights. If possible, schedule your sleep so it happens entirely at night. You'll fall asleep faster, stay asleep longer, and wake up feeling better.

Stay Consistent

Every time you fall asleep on your bedtime, your body adjusts to that time. Does that mean you have to say no to every single late-night event for the rest of your life? No. But it does mean you should default to "no." If evening activities are important to you, set a bedtime after them, clear your morning schedule, and invest in blackout shades or a sleep mask.

Arrange your sleep hours so you can do the things that really matter to you. Do them, then go to bed.

Take Back Screen Time

Your phone, tablet, computer, and TV screens mess with your sleep in many ways:

- Screens are designed to emit blue light to match the sun. Your mammal brain can't tell the difference.
- The rapid screen refresh (dozens of times per second) stimulates you.
- Whatever you're looking at is hard to look away from.

Screens keep you in a constant state of excitement and wakefulness. The best way to fight back is to spend the hour before bedtime doing something else, like reading a book under a yellow light.

The willpower cost to go that long without a screen may be unrealistic for the current version of you. If you must look at a screen for now, there are many ways to make it less stimulating so your poor mammal brain can fall asleep.

- Dim the brightness
- Use a blue light filter (comes built in on most phones)
- Switch to grayscale (black and white) mode
- Sit further away
- Turn off the other lights in your room

Most devices come with a setting that automatically turns on a blue light filter and reduces brightness (Apple calls it Night Shift). For your computer, check out justgetflux.com.

At the end of the day, remember that these changes are only *reducing* your willpower cost. You still need to spend some to turn everything off when your bedtime rolls around, get under the sheets, and close your eyes. Don't let the screen tell you whether or not you're tired. In 2021, screens are not the boss of you. 2021 is the year that you take back the night and give yourself the sleep you deserve.

Joseph Abell

Chapter 8
The Behavior Molecule

Navigating the Infinite

At any given moment, there are an endless list of things that you could be doing. Instead of reading this book, you could be texting random numbers asking for rice pilaf recipes. You could be playing Siamese Chess against yourself. You could be making a kite out of pages from your biology textbook.

You face those infinite possibilities every time you finish an activity. The options could be overwhelming, but they're not. That's because your mind has developed a sophisticated way to manage them so you can move from one activity to the next without slowing down: by grouping actions together into something I call a behavior molecule.

A behavior molecule is a cluster of connected actions suggested by a context.

Suppose you work as a museum janitor. As soon as you start work, you enter a behavior molecule. The atoms it holds are the things you're expected to do as a museum janitor. You wipe surfaces, sweep, mop, polish, and remove trash. When you finish one task, it doesn't occur to you that you could put on a suit of armor, climb the T-Rex skeleton, and pretend to be in a medieval version of Jurassic Park.

Your mind simply scans the molecule for the next activity suggested by the context.

In other words, you're not asking: "What should I do from the infinite possibilities before me?" You're asking: "What should I do from the set of behaviors in this molecule?"

You seamlessly switch to a different molecule when you clock out for your lunch break, and again when you return to work.

When you enter a familiar environment, you immediately default to those activities with almost no thought. This is most evident when you come home from school or work. You don't stand in the doorway making a pros and cons list. You automatically do five or six behaviors in a row like kicking off your shoes, putting away your keys, and hanging your mask. You've repeated these actions so many times that they have bonded together.

You probably spend most of your time within a behavior molecule. There's one you enter when you sit in the driver seat of your car. It contains driving, listening to music and podcasts, and talking on the phone. You enter another molecule when you enter your best friend's house. It has cooking together, deep conversations, and watching bad movies so you can make fun of them.

Leaving the Molecule

Not everything that you do happens inside a behavior molecule. You may sometimes cross into unfamiliar territory; something unexpected will happen or you'll break from the routine.

Suppose you're in a wedding party. You're driving alone to the ceremony when a tire suddenly goes flat. You pull over and check your map. Even if you change the tire immediately, you'll still be late to the ceremony. Do you change it anyway? Text and let them know you'll be late? Call a rideshare and come back for the car later? Jog the rest of the way?

This choice isn't like the many others you've already made that day. You have to be present and creative to figure out what to do next because you don't have any default behaviors for this unfamiliar situation. That is often stressful.

You know you're outside the molecule when you catch yourself thinking a lot about what to do next. Being outside a molecule for a long time can be overwhelming and exhausting, especially if you suffer from a lot of self-doubt.

Unbonded Behaviors

Your friend sent you her novel for review. You said you'd look it over, and you meant it. But now it's two weeks later and you haven't even opened it. You *intended* to. You had plenty of time in the last two weeks to do your usual scrolling and binging. Why didn't you open it? Because reviewing your friend's novel didn't fit into any of your current molecules. You never had a point in your day where reviewing the novel appeared as an option.

Whenever you say: "I've been meaning to do that," what you're really saying is: "My life doesn't have a molecule for that."

Remember, acting outside a molecule is stressful and exhausting. If you already have your day neatly divided into behavior molecules, growth is more involved than just adding new behaviors to the day.

Consider this schedule, sorted in terms of molecules:

- Wake up at the last possible second
- Get ready for work
- Drive
- Work
- Lunch
- Work
- Drive
- Dinner
- Scroll social media in front of the TV
- Bed

You decided to take up a daily yoga practice months ago. Your friend keeps talking about how great it is, and you keep sheepishly saying: "Yeah, I've been meaning to get started on that." But now, looking at your assorted molecules, you realize something: yoga doesn't fit into *any* of them.

If you don't change something big-picture, you'll continue to live day after day without even thinking about yoga. The few times that you do it will feel forced; they'll require enormous willpower because they exist outside of the molecule.

To implement lasting change, you'll need to build new molecules full of positive behaviors that are bonded together so they become as automatic as stepping through your front door.

Break the Bonds

Behaviors within a molecule are strongly bonded together. You move immediately from one to the next, often without even noticing that you've made a decision. If you decide to stop doing one of the behaviors in the middle of that molecule without changing anything else, you're in for a struggle.

You might be able to rearrange the molecule, so it works without the bad behavior. But you'll still have to constantly expend willpower to resist the default bonds in the molecule. It's like holding a cigarette in your hand and telling yourself that you won't light it.

Removing an entire molecule is easier than removing a single behavior within it.

Identify what that molecule is giving you and look for a new way to fill that need. Then build a brand new molecule full of intentional, positive behaviors.

Perhaps you spend an hour every evening gaming with a group of people that you don't respect. You're not fully present, you're not having a good time, and you're ashamed of the things they say that you tolerate. You could try to change your relationship with the group or spend less time gaming with them. That may help, but you're still fundamentally in the same molecule.

Instead, you realize that you're tolerating this molecule because you want to be part of a social group. You join a new group that convenes at the same time that you would have been gaming. Maybe you don't leave the clan entirely at first; you switch back and forth between the old and new groups. That's okay. Transition at the rate that your willpower allows. Just keep putting more time and attention into the new group until you're ready to leave the old one behind.

How to Build Good Molecules

Start with a single action that requires little willpower. Ideally, it's something easy that you enjoy doing.

When I started this process, I began with closing all the blinds in my home before bedtime – even the ones that weren't in my bedroom. My morning routine began with opening them all back up again. It was an easy task that required almost no willpower. It didn't do much by itself, but it laid the foundation for everything that came after.

Repeat that action until it's automatic. Then add a second behavior *immediately after the first one.*

Timing is critical.

If you give yourself a moment where you must decide what to do next, choosing the right thing will require more willpower.

Don't do that to yourself. Don't make yourself choose between meditation and creeping your ex's page. Don't pause for even a second, no matter how you feel. Tell yourself that you're not even consciously deciding to do it. You *already* decided, once and for all.

Grow your molecule by moving instantly from one behavior to the next. Every time you do that, the bonds between the behaviors strengthen. Eventually, the entire cluster will be automatic.

Morning & Evening Routines

Of all the behavior molecules in your life, these two are the most overlooked and the most important. Your morning routine sets the tone for your entire day and transitions you into your main productivity molecule – whatever that may be – with momentum. Your evening routine ensures that you'll get your critical night's sleep and creates a time in your schedule that you can engage in highly restorative behaviors.

This is something we see almost universally among the world's most successful people. Leaders, CEOs, celebrities, athletes, innovators, artists – if they're at the top of their field, you can bet they have specific morning and evening routines that they follow every single day. They're taking control of their time from the moment their alarm goes off. They're setting in motion a series of positive events.

To unlock unlimited willpower, you must do the same. It starts with simply saying: "I have a morning routine." Here's why that's so powerful.

The mere act of creating the right molecule suggests a buffet of healthy behaviors.

Here are a few behaviors you might put into a morning routine:

- Write in your dream journal
- Make your bed
- Go for a run
- Take a cold shower
- Drink lemon water
- Meditate
- Yoga
- Skin care routine
- Review your plan for the day
- Read non-fiction
- Clean your space

You may have seen lists like this before. You may even have tried to implement them but failed because you didn't have access to unlimited willpower. This time, you're going to succeed.

Assemble the Molecule Gradually

Remember: if you do something every single morning, it eventually becomes effortless. Create your morning routine with just *one thing* in it – something doable enough that you know you'll have enough willpower for it every single day, even when you're sleepy.

Here's how that might look.

In January, you decide to drink lemon water every morning. You lower the willpower cost by putting lemon juice in a prominent place in your fridge. You rename your alarm to "DRINK LEMON WATER," so it's the first thing you see when you wake up.

The alarm goes off. Instead of scrolling social media for a half hour, you immediately go to the kitchen and drink a glass of lemon water. You might be tempted to go further. But remember: you're not out to have one epic morning and then fall back into your old patterns.

You're going to have a lifetime of mornings that consistently get better and better.

So, even though you still have some willpower left, you let yourself do your default behavior. You're signaling to the tomorrow version of you that continuing this behavior is no big deal. Maybe you climb back into bed and scroll social media again. That's okay. Ascension doesn't happen in a day.

After two and a half months of lemon water, it's now completely automatic. You're ready for the next step: daily meditation.

You commit to meditating *as soon as you finish your lemon water.* You set a reminder for every evening to check your meditation spot to make sure it will be clean and ready for you. You rename your alarm "MEDITATE."

You start with a 60-second meditation. After a while, you build up to 2 minutes. Then 5. Now it's September, and you've built two positive habits that you'll continue doing automatically for the rest of your life. You're ready for the third thing: a skin care routine *as soon as you finish meditating*.

The Power of a Cup of Tea

You can use the same technique to build your evening routine. Evening has a unique challenge, however. You don't have to decide when to start your morning routine; you just wake up and you're in it. Your evening routine will require more willpower because you must stop doing something else – perhaps something stimulating that you do compulsively – to begin.

Remember the Arrival Hack from Chapter Four? Here's a specific version of it that I want you to try.

Drink a cup of herbal tea at the exact same time every evening.

That's it. Just drink a cup of tea! That's relaxing and requires minimal willpower. But once you start, you'll notice that you've transitioned into your evening molecule, and other evening activities become easier.

Many items in your evening routine – like taking out your contact lenses – are required to create the sleep opportunity we discussed in the previous chapter. Here are a few you might add when you're going strong:

- Journal
- Plan the next day
- Lay out tomorrow's outfit
- Prep your morning routine
- Read fiction
- Focus on something you're grateful for
- Stargaze

As with the morning routine, you'll need to pace yourself. Don't force yourself to do your ideal evening routine right after tea. If your willpower is utterly depleted, allow yourself to go right back to whatever you were doing before (for now). You'll get there. Be patient, and above all, be consistent.

More time is wasted in the evening than any other time of day. Commit. Set a reminder. Notice how the simple act of making and drinking tea changes the whole tone of your evening. Once it's automatic, you're ready to commit to doing something *immediately after your tea.*

You can use the molecule technique to transform your day into clusters of specific behaviors that you do one after the other, just like taking off your shoes and putting away your keys when you come home. Without having to stop and think, and without having to exert any willpower at all, you'll be living as your Ascended Self.

Chapter 9
The Virtuous Cycle

Let's put this all together. Here's how you use the principles in this book to live your best year ever.

Implement Doable Changes

You're not going to go from not working out at all to working out for an hour every single day. The willpower cost is just unrealistic. You'll burn out, give up, and feed your self-doubt. The good news: you don't have to get there all at once.

You just have to change your default behavior a little bit — and then keep changing it.

Find something so doable that you're confident you can incorporate it into your current life using your *current daily willpower surplus*. Perhaps that's working out for 20 minutes, 3 times a week. Perhaps it's just going to a gym for the first time. Find it and do it. Then do it again.

Every time you do it, it'll cost less willpower. It'll start to feel easy.

Then it'll feel normal.

Then it'll become automatic.

Since you have lots of willpower recharging and you're spending less and less of it each time, you'll find that you have more than you need. That means you're ready to make another change. You can turn up the heat on what you're already doing (longer/more frequent workouts, for example), or work on something else.

This is the Virtuous Cycle:

1. Identify a step toward your Ascended Self
2. Implement a doable change
3. Succeed and make it your permanent pattern
4. Teach yourself that you can change
5. Live in a way that you're proud of – but now you're more confident, and you can implement bigger changes

This technique works. It can change your life and allow you to blast through barriers that defeated you in the past. But it takes time and patience.

When you push through that first barrier, you're likely to get excited and start pushing the changes to an unsustainable level. You'll overwhelm yourself, deplete your willpower, and suffer setbacks. Watch out for this feeling, and when it comes: exercise restraint. You're not going to change your life overnight. You're going to change it a little bit every day for an entire year.

Learn as You Go

In 2021, you can access a vast library of knowledge about any topic, within seconds, for free, without getting off the couch. That's an incredible power that you should take advantage of constantly. Do your research before making a change. Don't just go on a juice cleanse because someone on Instagram did it; do the work and learn about healthy food choices (and then *don't* go on a juice cleanse).

You don't have to be an expert, but you should take responsibility for your choices and learn enough about them so that you can commit to them. The last thing you want to do is find out that you poured your limited time, resources, enthusiasm, and willpower into something that doesn't work – or worse yet, something that was harmful.

Get Help

If you can afford it, hire experts to help. Personal coaches, trainers, nutritionists, and interior designers won't do the work for you, but they can put you on the inside track to the best possible version of yourself. At the least, get help from your friend who already lifts or dresses well or knows about cars to help you make good choices in those areas.

Working regularly with professionals also introduces a level of accountability that greatly reduces willpower cost. It's much easier to practice piano when you know your tutor is coming in a few days to check your progress.

Experts are not an alternative to learning. Trust them, but don't blindly take their word if you can help it. Ask them to teach you about the choice so you can make an informed decision for yourself.

Harness, then Abandon Motivation

Think about the last motivational/self-help book you read. I'm guessing it made a lot of sense, and you felt inspired. Maybe you even recommended the book to some friends. But six months later, your life was basically unchanged. All that fire and clarity you felt when you finished the last page had faded.

Why? Were you just not motivated *enough*?

Perhaps you made too many changes at once and burned out. Or perhaps you didn't change at all because of your self-doubt. But there's another possible reason: you trusted your motivation, and it let you down.

Motivation is doing something because you feel like it. Discipline is doing something even though you don't feel like it.

The fact is this: feelings come and go. Sometimes you're fired up and energized, and other times you're exhausted. If you only do things when you feel like doing them, you will eventually stop doing anything that requires any amount of willpower.

Making good choices is easy when you're motivated. In fact, the hardest part is simply restraining your pace. But when the motivation fades, you need something else that will keep you on this path.

Depending on motivation is an invisible shackle that keeps most people from implementing real, lasting change.

Sure, you can chase the high again. You can listen to a speech or read a book or change your lock screen. You can pile wood onto the fire until it blazes bright. But eventually, as it always does, the fire will burn back down to ash. And you'll have the day that you really, really don't want to get off the couch. You won't even have the motivation to try to motivate yourself.

On that day, you will bargain with your Ascended Self. You'll tell yourself comforting little lies. "I deserve a break," you'll say. "I've been so good. I'm so overwhelmed. This is too hard. What difference does one day make? I'll get back on the bandwagon tomorrow."

That moment – that rainy day, sitting alone on the couch, feeling exhausted, with your favorite show waiting to be binged – *that* is the moment that defines you.

It's hard to identify life-defining moments when you're experiencing them. You expect them to be dramatic moments when everything stops, and all eyes are on you. But when you look back at the moments that mattered most, they'll be mundane. Uncomfortable. Lonely.

I remember a moment like that back in high school. I was up in the attic - the only place I was allowed to practice debate because my family was bothered by the noise. I paced in a small circle rehearsing my speech for the hundredth time. Dust swirled in the sunbeam cutting through the tiny window. It coated my throat, giving me a constant irritating scratch. The air was sweltering up there. I dripped sweat with every step.

There was a moment that I reached a tipping point of discomfort and exhaustion. The last of my motivation drained out of me, like the last sand in an hourglass. I stopped in my tracks and closed my eyes. I desperately wanted to go back downstairs and cool off. But I also knew that my speech wasn't ready yet. I knew that if I stopped now, I'd be letting myself down.

In that moment, I decided that I wasn't going to go back downstairs until my speech was ready, no matter how miserable I got. I still wasn't motivated. I was choosing to push *even though I didn't feel like it*. I took a deep breath, opened my eyes, and continued speaking.

At the time, that decision didn't seem like a big deal to me. But I look back on it now as one of the moments that define me as a person. I remember it more clearly than the roar of the crowd as I won a national championship a few months later.

If you let motivation be your master, you will stay on that couch as if you were chained to it. And it won't matter how good the little white lies you told yourself were: you'll have taught yourself, yet again, that you don't deserve your own trust.

But if you get off the couch anyway, you're saying that you're not a slave to your feelings. You're acting because you *choose* to act. You're honoring your commitment to yourself. You're choosing discipline instead of motivation. You're showing that can trust yourself no matter what your feelings are.

It's fine to be motivated, but please don't put stock in it. Enjoy it when it comes and let it go when it fades. Use your moments of motivation to identify what you want and make sustainable changes. Then settle in and stick to it. Keep grinding as the motivation fades away and the willpower cost rises. Get over that hill; use discipline to push your unmotivated self to the other side where the behavior is automatic.

No Exceptions Until It's Easy

Once something has become a part of your life, it's okay to make exceptions now and then. But during the first few weeks/months of a new behavior, you're vulnerable. You're still spending a lot of willpower because you're trying to change what feels familiar to you. During this time, compromising carries a terrible cost.

Suppose you've decided to stop eating fast food. The first two weeks are tough, but it's getting easier. Then you stay late at work and your boss announces that he's bringing the whole department fast food. Everyone else is giving him their food orders. You're tired and hungry. Chicken nuggets would really hit the spot right now. You start bargaining with your

Ascended Self. "I didn't mean I'll never eat fast food again, *ever*," you say to yourself. "It won't do any harm if I make an exception just for tonight."

But when your teeth sink into that chicken nugget, something terrible happens: *it feels familiar*. You remember that this is your true default. You're a fast food eater who has been pretending to be something else. And just like that, the willpower cost of avoiding fast food shoots back up again. It's like you're starting the process all over again – but it's worse now because you're discouraged. Avoiding fast food tomorrow will be even harder than day one.

If you stuck with it for long enough that fast food stopped feeling familiar, it'd be a different decision. Because then, indulging wouldn't move your default. You'd be able to enjoy it and then go back to your normal, nuggetless life. But you're not ready for that yet.

When you commit to something, *commit*. Stick with it no matter how hard or inconvenient it is. Don't do cheat days or skip the gym or hit the snooze button or go a penny over your budget or text your ex "just this once." See it through. You owe it to yourself to make your new behavior easy.

Cultivate Self-Efficacy

No one knows your struggle but you. What is automatic to someone else may be a massive personal triumph for you. When you achieve something, notice it! Acknowledge that you've succeeded and allow your beliefs about yourself to change.

Self-Efficacy is the belief that you can do what you choose to do.

Repeatedly failing at personal growth creates a generalized self-doubt, where you don't believe that you can change your situation. It pours cement into your shoes. It makes every future attempt at growth harder.

That means that your success is critical. If you're going to implement a change, you must see it through to its successful conclusion. You can't afford the memory of failure.

Repeatedly succeeding at personal growth has the exact opposite effect. Your confidence grows as you observe yourself making choices you respect. You stop thinking of yourself as a failure and realize that you are capable of anything. When you ponder the future, where the old you would have been filled with shame or doubt or fear or excuses, the new you – the one with unlimited willpower – is filled with excitement.

You know that you will succeed because you have already succeeded.

It's the only rational conclusion.

That feeling will build on its own, but you can accelerate the process by celebrating your successes. Maybe it seems small to everyone else. But to you, it's big. You decided to do something, and you followed through. You touched a barbell for the first time! You were sober for an entire week! You got in bed with lights off before midnight!

Notice yourself succeeding. Notice your beliefs about yourself changing. Notice your excitement growing.

Allow the self-doubt to fade away.

Chapter 10
Priorities

The potential of unlimited willpower can be overwhelming. You can change anything and become your Ascended Self! Where do you start?

Priorities are important. You want to move in a way that gives you the biggest results possible and sets you up for future success. The order you want to follow is divided into seven steps. Each has a few examples. These aren't hard-and-fast rules, they're just there to help you understand the step and get ideas for your own path.

1. Restorative Behaviors

These require willpower to implement, but rapidly recharge your willpower almost immediately. They give you a huge return on investment and set you up for everything else you want to do in your life. It's difficult to change anything else if you don't have strong willpower regeneration. So, start here.

- Sleep
- Meditate
- Take walks in the nearest park
- Restrict distracting, consumptive behaviors

2. The Thing You're Avoiding

You know what I'm talking about: the part of your life that drains you; that you talk about sheepishly; that you dread; that stresses you out when you think about it. The thing you know you need to change. You were hoping you could finish this book without thinking about it.

This is a tough area to produce change in, but it will have a positive ripple effect on everything else in your life – especially your self-respect. Don't wait. Once you have strong willpower generation, bring it to bear on this and deal with it.

- End a toxic relationship
- Quit smoking
- Clean your home and car
- Stop watching porn

3. Health

It's hard to overstate the importance of your physical well-being. You need your body to be in excellent shape to engage with every other part of your life. Spend your willpower creating a strong, healthy body that will take you wherever you want to go.

- Lift weights
- Cook good food
- Tackle chronic pain
- Do yoga

4. Money

If you're deep in debt or living paycheck-to-paycheck and can't afford things you really want, it's time to prioritize your finances. Money is a form of energy. If you don't have enough of it, you're living on battery-saver mode. You're missing out on everything that this life has to offer. And you're feeling a constant fear that you won't have enough to make it through. That weight drains you no matter what you're doing.

In contrast, having enough money allows you to radically change lives. Whatever you value highly – caring for others, owning cool stuff, making memories, travelling, changing the world, or just feeling safe – money will help you get there.

- Create a budget and stick to it
- Earn a degree in a lucrative field
- Change careers or start a new business
- Get a promotion/raise

You don't have to be wealthy to live a great life, but you shouldn't feel stressed or limited. Money has significant diminishing returns. A Princeton study suggested that, after about $75,000, increasing your annual income doesn't increase your happiness.[3]

Making more money won't count for much if it's making you more stressed, or if it's taking up so much of your life that you don't have time for rest, play, and human connection.

If you want to be a millionaire, go for it! But don't feel like you *have* to. The most-fulfilled version of you might only need a modest income that is spent wisely.

Make exactly as much money as you want – not a penny more or less.

5. Daily Surroundings

This isn't as shallow as it sounds. Your environment has a massive impact on your thoughts and feelings, as well as how you spend and recover willpower. Your daily items should charge you up every time you see or touch them. Create a lifestyle that you are proud of, and that you're proud to share with others.

- Update your wardrobe
- Repair or throw away everything that's broken
- Move
- Decorate your home
- Upgrade your gear

6. Mental Stuff

Expand your knowledge and experience. Challenge yourself to see what's over the horizon. What does your Ascended Self know that you don't?

- Learn a new skill
- Create art
- Take up a hobby

7. Love & community

Do you have the social, family, romantic, and sex life you want? If not, why? Learn what's holding you back and get after it.

- Build a healthy long-term relationship
- Surround yourself with positive people
- Start conversations with strangers
- Adopt a pet

The most common reason people don't have the connections they want is self-doubt.

Perhaps you want to be part of a vibrant friend group that confides in and comes through for each other. To do that, you have to go out and find positive, reliable people. To do *that*, you have to believe that you're worthy of being their friend.

Perhaps you want to be in a happy, passionate romance. To do that, you need to meet attractive people. To do *that*, you need to believe that you are worthy of spending time with them.

There are plenty of self-help books that tell you to "fake it until you make it" – for example, just keep approaching people until you are numb to the pain of rejection. That ignores the real problem.

You don't fix self-doubt by failing so much that you don't notice it anymore, you fix it by fixing yourself.

This is why Love & Connection isn't the first item on the list. Get your life in order first! Earn your self-respect; become someone who has a lot to offer. Then you'll notice that talking to others isn't so difficult.

The fact is, you *can* fake it – up to a point. But you're never going to experience the genuine connections you crave if you haven't built yourself into a strong, positive, high-energy person.

Imagine your Ascended Self again:

- You get plenty of sleep.
- You meditate.
- You consume and look at screens intentionally.
- You don't do things you're ashamed of.
- You have as much money as you want.
- You're active.
- You eat and dress well.
- All your stuff works.
- You have hobbies.
- You're learning new things.
- You're excited for each new day.

We're talking about somebody that anyone would be lucky to be around.

A byproduct of growing into your Ascended Self is becoming irresistible.

You'll seek out the company of others not so they can distract you from the dark cloud swirling around you, but because you have so much awesomeness that you just have to share it. You'll find that people don't need to be tricked into being around you. You'll radiate genuine confidence and joy and enthusiasm.

So: you don't need techniques, and you don't need to pretend. All you need is unlimited willpower.

Joseph Abell

Chapter 11
An Ascended World

Self-Doubt Society

Real life isn't like a cartoon, where people are either Good or Bad. *Everyone* wants to be better and live in a better world. But everyone also fails, and every time they do, the cloud of self-doubt gets thicker. Most people have failed so much that they have given up on their Ascended Selves completely.

We live in a society full of people who have given up. Their shame makes them defensive. Their disappointment makes them jealous. Their fear makes them angry. Their exhaustion makes them desperate. Their poverty makes them selfish. Instead of growing and serving and creating, they have devoted their lives to distractions.

The fact that even a single person's potential goes wasted is a tragedy. The fact that we live in a world full of such waste is heartbreaking.

We could live in a world of Ascended Selves – one in which every single person becomes who they are supposed to be. What would a such a society look like?

- War, violence, and crime would vanish.
- Everyone would have everything they needed to thrive.
- Science would surge forward.
- Nature and civilization would flourish side-by-side.
- Each moment would be full of joy.

- Love and unity would be magnified on an unimaginable level.

Of course, we won't see that in our lifetimes. But we can create glimpses of it. We can lead by example. We can create a smaller version of it that fills the room, or the building, or the block. We can surround ourselves with people who ascend with us. We can master ourselves and become a shining light that turns back darkness.

All it takes to create the Ascended World is for each of us to stand at the base of the mountain, look up, begin to climb – and then to continue climbing, making sustainable changes, building willpower reserves and self-efficacy with each step.

Your Last First Step

Your Ascended Self is not a hypothetical perfect person. It's you at your best. It is, by definition, *attainable*. When you start this journey, it may seem like an abstract concept. But the closer you get, the more real it will become. Your Ascended Self will take form in front of you, like an old friend stepping out of heavy fog. You'll work hard. You'll make tough choices. You'll trade excuses for self-respect. And then one day, you'll wake up and look in the mirror and see your Ascended Self smiling back at you.

That can happen for you. It *will* happen. It *must*.

The time has come for you to return to that mountain and, for the very last time, begin to climb.

The journey to become a citizen of the Ascended World is long, difficult, and often lonely. But you can and must make it. Never lose sight of the person you can be. Never lose sight of how different your life can become within a single year.

You can become an exceptional person. You can unlock unlimited willpower.

Now lower this book and ascend.

Reference

[1] Zach McCann, Sleep tracking brings new info to athletes, ESPN, June 1, 2012.

[2] Centers for Disease Control and Prevention, 1 in 3 adults don't get enough sleep, February 8, 2016.

[3] Daniel Kahneman and Angus Deaton, High income improves evaluation of life but not emotional well-being, Princeton University, August 4, 2010

Printed in Great Britain
by Amazon

25183251R00076